Anacondas

By Christy Steele

Raintree Steck-Vaughn Publishers

A Harcourt Company

Austin · New York
www.steck-vaughn.com

ANIMALS OF THE RAIN FOREST

Published by Raintree Steck-Vaughn Publishers, an imprint of Steck-Vaughn Company.

Library of Congress Cataloging-in-Publication Data
Steele, Christy.
    Anacondas/by Christy Steele.
        p.cm. -- (Animals of the rain forest)
        ISBN 0-7398-3099-6
        1. Anacondas--Juvenile literature. [1. Anacondas. 2. Snakes] I. Title.
II. Series

QL666.O63 S74 2000
597.96--de21   00-33815

Printed in the United States of America
10 9 8 7 6 5 4 3 2 1 W 02 01 00

Produced by Compass Books

Photo Acknowledgments
All photographs by Bill Holmstrom and E. Dickstein (page 18), courtesy of the Wildlife Conservation Society, headquartered at the Bronx Zoo, New York

Content Consultant
Bill Lamar
Field Naturalist and Herpetologist
Adjunct Professor of Biology, University of Texas, Tyler
Read Bill's biography online at—
http://www.greentracks.com/TourLeaders.html

Contents

Range of the
Anaconda

A Quick Look at Anacondas

What do anacondas look like?
Anacondas are the heaviest snakes in the world. All three kinds of anacondas have patches of black, brown, yellow, orange, or brown covering their bodies.

Where do anacondas live?
Anacondas live in South America. They live near water in grasslands and rain forests.

What do anacondas eat?
Anacondas eat meat. They catch and eat fish and animals, such as small deer, pigs, and rodents.

Do anacondas have any enemies?
Adult anacondas have few natural enemies. At times, caimans or jaguars may attack small anacondas.

An anaconda's dark markings help it blend in with its surroundings.

Anacondas in the Rain Forest

Anacondas are the heaviest snakes in the world. Large females can be several feet thick and weigh up to 500 pounds (227 kg). They may grow up to 30 feet (9 m) long or more. Most females are around 20 feet (6 m) long. Male anacondas are smaller than females. They usually are 7 to 10 feet (2 to 3.5 m) long. They weigh less than 50 pounds (22 kg).

There are three types of anacondas. Each type has different colors and markings. Green anacondas are olive-green. Yellow anacondas are yellow or tan. The de Schauensee's or blotched anaconda has big dark spots on its back. All three kinds have bands of black, brown, reddish, or orange on their heads. Patches of black, brown, yellow, orange, or brown cover their bodies.

Where Anacondas Live

Anacondas live in and around the rain forests of South America. Many anacondas live in Amazonia. This is the largest rain forest in the world. It grows around the Amazon River.

Different kinds of anacondas live in different places. Green anacondas live in most parts of northern and central South America. Yellow anacondas live only in Argentina, southern Brazil, and Paraguay. Blotched anacondas live in northeast South America.

Anacondas can live on land or in the water. Anacondas live near freshwater rivers, lakes, and muddy streams. They also live in flooded forests, wet grasslands, and swamps.

Rainy Season and Dry Season

Anacondas have large home ranges. A home range is a special space that anacondas know well. Anacondas move around their home ranges to look for food and water. An anaconda goes to certain places in its range during each season. There is a dry season and a rainy season in the rain forest.

▲ **Anacondas sometimes rest in burrows made by other animals.**

Little rain falls during the dry season. Water may be hard to find. Then anacondas spend a great deal of time near drying pools of water.

Much rain falls during the rainy season. Rivers rise. Water floods the forest floor and grasslands. Anacondas travel most during the rainy season. They spend time swimming through flooded forests and grasslands.

The underside of every anaconda has many light and dark scales. These markings are different on each snake.

Reptiles

Anacondas are reptiles. Reptiles are cold-blooded animals. Cold-blooded animals have blood that is about the same temperature as the air or water around them. Temperature is how hot or cold something is. Anacondas lie in the sun or rest on tree branches to warm their bodies. They swim or bury themselves in mud to cool themselves.

Hard body coverings help keep a reptile safe. Colorful scales protect an anaconda's body. Scales are thick pieces of skin. Clear scales even cover an anaconda's eyes.

Special Body Parts

Anacondas use large scales called scutes to travel on land. A row of scutes covers the underside of an anaconda. The anaconda presses its scutes into the ground to push and pull itself along.

Anacondas have about 100 sharp teeth. The teeth point toward the inside of anacondas' mouths. The shape of the teeth helps anacondas bite and hold on to prey. Prey are animals an anaconda hunts and eats.

Special jaws help an anaconda eat large prey. Its lower jaw is divided in the middle of the chin. This lets it open its mouth wide. A stretchy band of tough skin connects to the hinges of the upper and lower jawbone. The snake can stretch this special ligament to open its mouth very wide.

An anaconda is killing a bird by squeezing it.

Hunting and Eating

Anacondas are carnivores. They eat only meat. They catch and eat other animals. Young anacondas eat different things than adult anacondas do. Young anacondas are not as fast or strong as adult anacondas. They cannot catch large animals.

Young anacondas eat a great deal of fish. They also eat small animals, such as frogs, lizards, birds, and turtles. Adult anacondas eat small deer, caimans, and rodents. These small animals have two large front teeth. Sometimes they eat ocelots and young jaguars. These animals are in the cat family.

Anacondas can go a long time without eating. One meal can last an anaconda several months. The anaconda may eat only four or five times a year.

Anacondas often swim along the water's edge to hunt.

Hunting

Anacondas usually hunt in the water. They move faster in water than they do on land. An anaconda's heavy body floats in water, so it can swim quickly. On land, an anaconda has to work hard to pull its heavy body along. Prey often outruns an anaconda on land.

Anacondas hunt by sneaking up on their prey. They swim with only their eyes and nostrils above water. This makes it hard for prey to see them. Anacondas sometimes hide under floating plants and leaves as they swim. Other times, they swim near the water's shore. They wait for birds or animals to drink the water. Then they catch the animals.

An anaconda strikes once it has found prey. It can strike up to 20 feet (6 m) in one second. The snake then sinks its teeth into the prey. It wraps its body around the animal while its teeth hold the prey. All this happens very quickly. An anaconda can catch prey in less than one second.

Sometimes anacondas pull their prey underwater. They hold it underwater until the prey drowns. Other times, anacondas tightly squeeze their bodies around their prey. The hold is so tight that their prey cannot breathe. The prey's blood also stops flowing. Prey usually dies within a minute or two.

▲ **Anacondas can eat up to 95% of their body weight. This anaconda is resting while its food digests.**

Eating

Anacondas do not chew their food. They swallow their food whole. First, they stretch their jaw ligaments to open the hinges of their jaws. This allows them to eat animals larger than themselves.

Anacondas usually swallow the prey's head first. This way, the prey's limbs fold together inside the anaconda. Otherwise, the limbs could spread and hurt the anaconda.

It may take an anaconda several hours to swallow very large prey. Swallowing makes the anaconda tired. An anaconda is more open to attack when it is swallowing or breaking down its food. It is unable to fight if its mouth is full. An anaconda will spit out its food if it feels it is in danger.

Special juices in an anaconda's body break down the bones and beaks of prey. It may take one week or more for all of the food to digest. Until it does, the anaconda's body will have a large bulge in it. This bulge is what is left of the body of its prey.

Anacondas must break down their food as quickly as possible. If they do not, the food will begin to rot. Rotting food will kill the anaconda if it cannot digest it fast enough.

Anacondas use their tongues to find special scents from other anacondas.

An Anaconda's Life Cycle

Anacondas grow for several years before they are adults. They mate every couple of years as soon as they are fully grown.

Anacondas mate during the end of the dry season. Their young are born during the rainy season. Young anacondas can hide from enemies among leaves in flooded forests. At this time, they can also catch newly hatched fish and other animals.

Anacondas live and hunt alone. They come together only during mating season. Female anacondas give off special scents, or smells, to find males. Male anacondas can smell these scents from up to 3 miles (5 km) away. Males will travel a long way to reach females.

Anacondas in a mating ball like this one may stay wrapped around each other for up to six weeks.

Mating Balls

Anacondas make a mating ball once a male has found a female. A mating ball is a female anaconda with one or more males wrapped around her.

The snakes in mating balls hide themselves by staying partly buried in the mud. Sometimes they hide under plants or grass near water holes. After mating, the snakes return to their home ranges.

Giving Birth

Instead of laying eggs, females hold their eggs within their bodies. Each egg is soft and clear. Large females may have around 70 eggs. Smaller anacondas have 30 to 50 eggs. Young anacondas grow inside these eggs. They eat the yolk from the eggs.

Females often lie in the sun while they are carrying eggs. The sun warms the eggs. It makes the new anacondas inside the eggs grow faster. The eggs hatch inside the female during the rainy season. Then the female gives birth.

▲ The mother anaconda will soon leave this newborn anaconda.

Dangers

The female leaves her young after they are born. The young must care for themselves. Very few newborn anacondas live to be adults. Many die within the first few months of life.

Animals such as birds, piranhas, and caimans eat young anacondas. Young anacondas are weak. They hide from enemies instead of fighting back. An anaconda becomes stronger as it grows older. Very few animals will try to kill an adult anaconda.

Molting

Anacondas must shed their skin to grow. This is called molting.

Over time, an anaconda will grow too big for its old skin. New skin begins growing underneath the old skin. The old skin may become dull.

The anaconda is ready to molt as soon as its new skin is fully grown. The new skin pushes against the old skin and loosens it. The anaconda may rub against rocks or sticks to help pull off the old skin. Then the anaconda crawls out of its old skin.

Over time, this new skin will become too small as well. Then the anaconda molts again.

Most anacondas hide if they see people coming near.

Living with Anacondas

People have always been careful around anacondas. Some native Amazonians believe anacondas have special powers. They will not harm anacondas because they believe the snakes could hurt them.

Over the years, people have told many untrue stories about anacondas. In the 1940s, a newspaper story said that a 156-foot (47.5-m) long anaconda fought army soldiers and knocked over buildings. In 1997, people made a movie about huge anacondas that hunted and ate people.

Most anacondas in the wild stay away from people. There are many stories about anacondas eating people. But most of the stories have proven to be untrue.

Studying Anacondas

Scientists have only begun to study anacondas within the past 10 years. Studying these snakes can be hard work. Anacondas live in hard-to-reach places in the rain forest. The snakes often hide.

Some scientists walk through grasslands barefoot to find anacondas. They catch anacondas to measure and weigh them. Then they put small radio transmitters on the snakes. These machines tell scientists where the anacondas go. This helps scientists learn about anacondas' home ranges and where they hunt.

Anacondas in Danger

Many people hunt anacondas for their skins. They make things like wallets and shoes out of anaconda skins. Some people catch anacondas and sell them as pets. Today, some people are making laws against hunting and selling anacondas.

People also put anacondas in danger when they cut down the rain forest. Some people do this to make room for farms and roads.

▲ Scientists catch anacondas to study them.
Then they release them again.

Anacondas could be lost forever if the rain
forest is destroyed. If anacondas die out, other
plants and animals could be hurt, too. Without
anacondas to eat them, the number of animals
in the rain forest would increase. The animals
would eat too many plants. Anacondas and all
the living things in the rain forest work together
to keep the rain forest healthy.

Glossary

Amazonia (am-uh-ZONE-ee-uh)—the largest rain forest in the world

carnivore (KARN-i-vor)—an animal that only eats other animals

cold-blooded (kohld-BLUHD-id)—having blood that is about the same temperature as the air or water

molting (MOHLT-ing)—shedding an outer skin in order to grow

prey (PRAY)—animals that are hunted by other animals for food

rainy season (RAY-nee SEE-suhn)—a time of several months where it rains almost every day in the rain forest; forests and grasslands flood during the rainy season.

scales (SKAYLS)—small pieces of thick, hard skin

scute (SKYOOT)—a large scale on the underside of some animals; an anaconda uses its scutes to pull itself along on the ground.

Internet Sites and Addresses

Anaconda Printout: Enchanted Learning
http://www.enchantedlearning.com/subjects/
   reptiles/snakes/Anacondacoloring.shtml

Planet Anaconda
http://www.planetpets.simplenet.com/
   plntanac.htm

Rain Forest Alliance
http://www.rainforest-alliance.org

Anaconda Project
Wildlife Conservation Society
2300 Southern Boulevard
Bronx, NY 10460-1099

Rain Forest Action Network
221 Pine Street, Suite 500
San Francisco, CA 94104

Index